Investing in Ethereum

A Simple, Concise & Complete Guide to Investing in the New Cryptocurrency Ethereum

Table of Contents

Introduction 4
Chapter 1: Why Ethereum Matters 6
Chapter 2: Understanding Ethereum Basics 11
Chapter 3: A Step-by-Step Guide to Using
Ethereum 17
Chapter 4: Smart Contracts and Ethereum
Integration 24
Chapter 5: Becoming Acquainted with How
Ethereum is Mined 29
Chapter 6: Ethereum Versus Bitcoin 35
Chapter 7: Investing in Ethereum 40
Chapter 8: Top Tips to Make Your Ethereum
Experience Better 45
Chapter 9: The Pros and Cons of Ethereum Use 49
Chapter 10: Ethereum and the Future Potential of
Cryptocurrency 54
Conclusion 59

Introduction

For your convenience we have compiled a list of websites which will be of interest to those interested in Ethereum: *www.wisereachday.com/ethereum*

Congratulations for downloading this book, *Investing in Ethereum:A Simple, Concise & Complete Guide to Investing in the New Cryptocurrency Ethereum*. Thank you for doing so.

This book is going to fully educate you on the cryptocurrency that is Ethereum. You may have heard of an alternative to Ethereum known as Bitcoin, but know little about cryptocurrency in general. Conversely, you may already be knowledgeable about Bitcoin, and feel as if you're ready to learn about other types of cryptocurrency that currently exist. Regardless of your exact reasons for investing your time into what this book has to offer, rest assured that after reading this book, you will completely understand what Ethereum is, how using Ethereum can benefit your life, and how Ethereum differs from other key cryptocurrencies that are popular on the market today.

While we will briefly discuss how cryptocurrencies and the technology behind them are changing the way that the public interacts with trust in both their banks and their marketplace, the majority of this book will be dedicated solely to Ethereum. As a global consumer, you should have an inherent interest in how currency is changing in the age of the internet. As the world's money and the world's resources seem to be constantly exchanged more quickly, understanding developing technologies will ensure that the way in which you seek wealth is able to evolve and sustain itself. This is why understanding Ethereum is important.

There are plenty of books on the market related to this topic, again thank you for choosing this one! Enjoy the rest of what this book can offer your life.

Chapter 1: Why Ethereum Matters

Before getting into the basic concepts surrounding Ethereum and how to operate within this technology, it's important to understand why Ethereum is important and what it means for society as a whole. As with most inventions and innovations, Ethereum was born out of a societal need that was not being met. This chapter will briefly discuss that need and will also touch on blockchain technology as a whole, it being the technology enabling platforms like Ethereum to function. We will end this chapter discussing how Ethereum differs from other types of popular cryptocurrencies, as this will pave the way for conceptualizing the following concepts presented in this book.

Eroded Trust in Banking Institutions

Prior to the 2008 economic collapse, people generally had trust in their banks. The privatized structure of a bank largely allowed bank consumers to feel as if their money was being handled with both respect and transparency. When the economy fell and the banks were ousted as being filled with employees who were being enticed to hide information from their customers, it suddenly became clear that the banks did not entirely deserve the trust the public had given them. While poor and deceptive investment decisions (especially in the housing market) largely led to the economic collapse of 2008, the takeaway feeling that rippled through the public after thousands of homeowners went into foreclosure was that their banks had lied to them. This prompted the public to take back the trust it had given these banks. It's at this point when cryptocurrency made its debut.

The Emergence of Ethereum

While bitcoin was the first official cryptocurrency to make its way to the digital marketplace, Ethereum was actually created by a man who was working for bitcoin when it was first developed. His name was Vitalik Buterin. Bitcoin was developed in 2009, and Ethereum was not officially launched until early 2014. As you can see, Buterin had quite a bit of time to fully understand the blockchain technology behind Bitcoin, prior to launching Ethereum. As of June 2017, Ethereum has netted over 400 million dollars in profit, and it's also notable that multiple foreign entities have endorsed the platform. Both Japan and Russia have publicly endorsed Ethereum's capabilities. These international entities are a primary reason why the popularity of the Ethereum has increased so rapidly.

Decentralization and Blockchain

Without going into too many specifics about how blockchain technology works, it's important to understand that Ethereum and other cryptocurrencies like it are all supported by blockchain technology. At its core, blockchain technology enables untraditional banking systems to exist through the notion of decentralization. In other words, when it comes to traditional monetary transactions, a bank is considered to be a third party who is involved with making sure that two people exchange their money safely. For example, if you are looking to give your friend Joe money to cover the cost of a camping trip you planned, you may decide to give him this money you owe him in the form of a check. Without the bank's help, this money that this check represents would not be able to be transferred into money in Joe's account. The bank processes the check for you, and makes this transaction with your friend possible.

With cryptocurrencies, you don't need to use a bank. Instead of trusting one bank or single institution with your money, you instead trust a network of multiple authoritative and mathematically reinforced administrators. All of these administrators must agree that your transaction is correct prior to it being approved. This is what lies at the heart of the blockchain technology. By dispersing the trust that's typically involved when you transfer money through a bank, more transparency is possible. Not only that, but a typical blockchain application will also provide you with a ledger. This ledger is able to keep track of every single transaction that occurs within the blockchain system. This way, everything that occurs within the blockchain is documented and can be easily found if and when needed.

Beyond Counting Coins

One of the biggest reasons why Ethereum is becoming arguably one of the most reputable forms of cryptocurrency on the market right now is because its platform goes beyond currency. Trust in a marketplace can extend from currency to mortgage ownership to marital status. In other words, non-monetary transactions are the primary transactions that Ethereum targets. While Ethereum does have its own type of cryptocurrency known as Ether, it uses what are known as Smart Contracts to complete and solidify contractual agreements between parties without any physical human intervention. By setting up the contract parameters within the Smart Contract, the person signing the legal document is then bound to the terms within it. It's important to understand that even though Ethereum differs from other types of cryptocurrency platforms that currently exist, all of these cryptocurrencies are operated through blockchain technology.

This expansion of blockchain to include contractual agreements between parties is a major reason why Ethereum is currently receiving so much attention. From a corporate perspective, being able to send someone a document to fill out rather than formally meet with someone will save money because these companies will likely have less employees to hire. With less people to hire, there is much less room for human error. Additionally, with less room for error, greater efficiency and accuracy is possible. Lastly, unlike with bitcoin, Ethereum allows you to actually create your own blockchain networks. This means that you are able to develop your own currency, your own terms of ownership, and your own contractual obligation requirements. Ethereum is thus much more adaptable to an individual's ownership preferences and requirements when it comes to running a business or operating a network for a small niche of people. Bitcoin, contrastingly, was the first blockchain network to successfully function, but is only capable of allowing people to trade funds.

At this point, you should have a working understanding of how Ethereum came to emerge within a society where trust in the marketplace was at an all-time low. It can also be argued that the emergence of Bitcoin ultimately led to the introduction of Ethereum as a concept and digital tool. This book will get into more detail regarding how Bitcoin and Ethereum differ, but it's important to understand that the question of whether Bitcoin or Ethereum will outperform the other is still largely unanswered. A primary reason why cryptocurrencies are so exciting is because the future of this technology is still largely unknown. Questions regarding security, duplicity, and accessibility still need to be figured out. It seems that the only way to truly answer these questions is to wait until the boundaries that surround cryptocurrency in general are tested.

Chapter 2: Understanding Ethereum Basics

Now that you have been provided with an idea of the climate surrounding Ethereum's emergence and what makes Ethereum distinct from other types of cryptocurrencies that are on the market, we will now begin to work towards developing your intricate understanding of what Ethereum is and how it functions. After reading this chapter, you will have a working definition of all the major aspects of Ethereum. You will also be given information regarding multiple types of currency that exist within Ethereum, and the controversy surrounding these various currency types. This way, you will know exactly what type of currency to purchase if and when you decide to invest in Ethereum.

The Ether Currency

Perhaps the most rudimentary term integral to the Ethereum network is its currency, known as ether. Without owning any ether, you will be unable to operate anything on Ethereum's platform. In other words, ether is what an Ethereum user will purchase if he or she is looking to participate within the Ethereum network. You can compare this to having to buy a subway pass prior to traveling to various places in New York City. You want to send yourself from point A to point B, but you cannot do this without first subscribing to the subway system in the form of payment. Unlike a train network, the cost of 1 ether is going to depend on the demand for the currency itself. Right now, 1 ether is going to cost you around $225. If you're interested in purchasing ether, you can either find a physical exchange place where ether is sold, or you can mine the currency itself. We will get into more detail about mining in a moment. On the other hand, some websites where you can purchase ether with US dollars include Coinbase, Gemini, or Kraken. Please keep in mind that these sites are going to require that you verify your information via identification documents prior to being given access to the ether coin. Still, it might make sense to at least check out these websites prior to purchasing any ether at all.

The Notion of Mining

Similar to when the people of the Wild West mined for gold, ether also must be digitally mined. This is not done with a shovel or chisel, but rather through cryptographic puzzles that must be solved. As was stated previously, a blockchain network is comprised of multiple computers who all collectively use their authority to verify transactions. The people behind these computers are known as miners. An additional duty that the miners have is to extract ether through cryptographic puzzles. Not only do these puzzles ensure that new ether is being created; it also helps to secure Ethereum network from hackers through encryption upkeep. A primary reason why mining is necessary is so that double spending is more difficult. Because miners are mathematically verifying that the transactions that are taking place are true, it's more difficult for anyone using the network to illegally spend the same ether twice.

Hash Functions

Also known as a hash algorithm, this is mathematical equation that the miners must solve when attempting to upload new ether to the Ethereum network or upload a block of transactions to the blockchain. Hash functions are integral to any blockchain network, but the hash equations themselves are going to differ depending on the blockchain network you're using. On average, hash functions take about ten minutes to solve. The goal of solving a hash function is to produce a nonce number. A nonce number can be defined as a predefined number that the miner is looking for while solving the hash function. In exchange for utilizing a lot of their own computer space and solving these hash functions as quickly as possible, a miner is typically going to be paid in some fashion. Within Ethereum, this means that the miners receive ether in exchange for their hard work supporting the system as a whole.

Smart Contracts

An entire chapter of this book is dedicated to the ins and outs of Smart Contracts; however, Smart Contracts are so integral to Ethereum operation that they need to at least be mentioned here. A Smart Contract can be best defined as a digital agreement between two parties. Similar to a financial transaction, a Smart Contract allows two parties to involve themselves in a transaction, without necessarily relying on one another for the deal to complete itself. For example, let's say that Bob is looking to sell his home. Sally decides that she wants to buy Bob's home. If you've ever purchased a home in the past, then you already know that the paperwork involved with this task can be painstakingly boring. A Smart Contract essentially fast-tracks this process for you. In other words, in the physical world, all Sally and Bob would have to do is agree upon a date for the Contract to begin. Once that date arrives, the Smart Contract would automatically engage, at which point it would notify both Sally and Bob of its completion. Again, we will go much deeper into Smart Contracts in a subsequent chapter.

Dapps

Dapps is an abbreviation that stands for decentralized application. The best way to describe a Dapps is to first think about how a typical application works. An application that is open on your phone, for example, can only operate when it's running on a central server. In other words, only a few computers are able to run the application. Contrastingly, a Dapps application is designed to operate on only decentralized computers. Therefore, these applications are designed to work on the computers that the miners use along the Ethereum blockchain.

Swarms and Whispers

Within Ethereum, the goal is to have the network operate as a global computer. Ideally, any decentralized computer that's been programmed to run Ethereum should be able to reach it. While the blockchain technology behind Ethereum largely enables any computer to talk to one another, the Smart Contracts that are integral to the Ethereum application require excess storage for two crucial reasons. Firstly, the Smart Contracts need to remember the parameters of the Contracts that are being signed. If there's limited storage space, memory is limited. Secondly, in order to communicate properly across the Dapps, each decentralized computer needs to have enough bandwidth to do so.

To compensate for these needs that the Smart Contracts have, the concepts of swarms and whispers were produced. The swarm acts as the storage that allows for greater memory, while the whispers provide the greater bandwidth that the Smart Contracts require. The image below should provide greater clarity for these concepts:

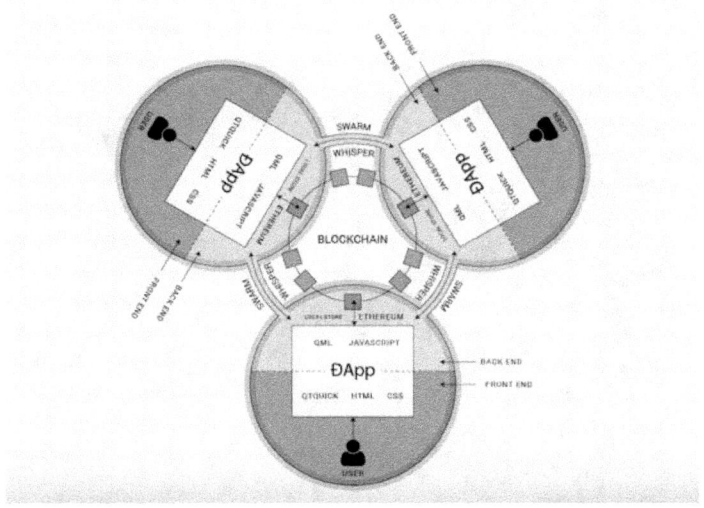

The three circles in this image represent three separate decentralized computers. As you can see, both the swarms and the whispers have been strategically placed to connect all of the Dapps to one another. You can also see that both the swarms and the whispers are placed in what's known as the "back end" of the Dapps. The back end is the decentralized aspect of the Dapps. In other words, a Dapps computer is programmed so that it's essentially cut into half. The front end of the computer houses the centralized Ethereum network. The CSS, HTML, and QTQUICK code all contain the information that is essential for the Ethereum website to run, while the back end of the computer communicates with the front end of the computer through the points where the swarms and the whispers interact.

Chapter 3: A Step-by-Step Guide to Using Ethereum

At this point, you know essentially what Ethereum is. You know that you can't operate Ethereum without ether, and that an ether coin currently costs around $225. This next chapter is going to provide you with information regarding what you have to do in order to use Ethereum in a step-by-step fashion. After reading this chapter, you will know exactly the steps that you need to take in order to set up an Ethereum platform on your own computer.

Step 1 to Using Ethereum: Get Your Ether

Before anything else, the first thing that you need to do in order to start using Ethereum is to get yourself some ether. The easiest way to do this is to simply head to Gemini, Coinbase, or any other website that sells ether. Next, create a login for yourself and link your debit card to the account. After your debit card account has been verified, you will then be able to buy and sell ether at your leisure.

Step 2 to Using Ethereum: Download an Ethereum Mist Wallet

After you have your ether account setup, the next step is to download an Ethereum Mist wallet to your computer. It's important to make sure that you download the most recent version of the wallet code, so that you don't end up running into any unanticipated problems. Once your wallet is downloaded, you'll be able to send, receive, and store ether coins on your computer. Along with making sure that you're downloading the most recent version of code, you also want to make sure that you download the version of the wallet that is compatible with your computer. It wouldn't make any sense to download the Apple version of code when you own a PC. To find this code, a simple Google search for "most recent Ethereum Mist wallet download" or something along those lines.

Step 3 to Using Ethereum: Install the Ethereum Mist Wallet

Once you've found the code for which you're looking and have downloaded it to your computer, the next step is to allow the program to install. As it's installing, you are going to see a dialog box that resembles the following:

As you can see, there is a lot of information downloading to your computer. Patience is key while you're waiting for the node to finish its install. Once completed, you will then see the following screen:

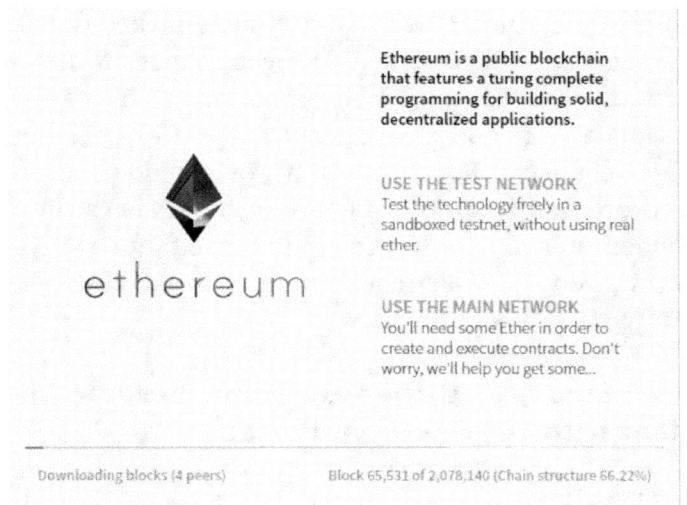

While the previous screen was downloading Ethereum's nodes, you can see at the bottom of this screen that the blocks of Ethereum's blockchain will download at this point. At this point, you will also be prompted to choose whether you'd like to launch Ethereum with your own network, or whether you'd like to test the platform on a network where your personal ether will not have to be used. It's highly recommended that you choose to launch Ethereum through the test network initially. As you can see, if for some reason you have not purchased any ether for yourself prior to completing this step, you will still have time to do so after this step has been completed.

Step 4 to Using Ethereum: Create Your Password

As with most other types of accounts that you can create online, once Ethereum has finished downloading, you will be asked to create a password for your account. It's extremely important to recognize that once you choose a password, you will *never* be able to change it. For this reason, you should choose a password that is not only memorable, but also strong. You definitely do not want to put yourself into a situation where your wallet ends up being hacked because your password is too basic.

Step 5 to Using Ethereum: Become Familiar with Your Account Portal

After you've created your password, you will then be able to access your account's home page. This page is going to resemble the following image:

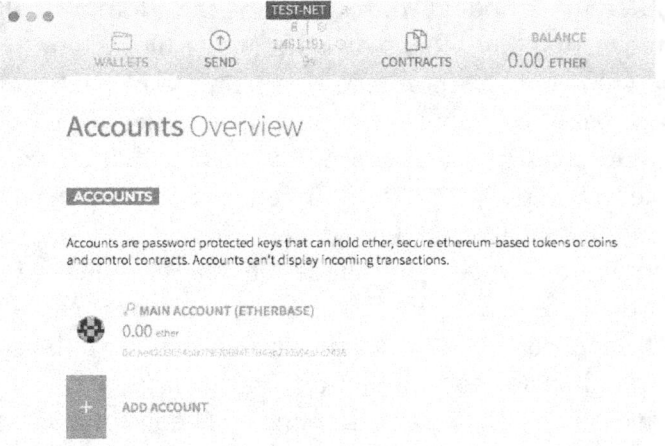

As you can see, your account will have your wallet, your contracts, and the option to send ether at the top of its menu. You also have the option of adding additional accounts to your ether profile under the same username that you've already created. This way, you're able to send and receive various types of currency, since you are able to turn your ether into any type of currency that you'd like. Remember, Ethereum allows you to choose the type of currency that you'd like to make your ether.

In the image above you can also see the number of nodes that Ethereum has accumulated in real time (this number is located below the red "Test Net"). If your Ethereum software stops working, you'll know because the number of nodes in the network will stop populating itself or this number will turn into a zero. If this does occur, you will probably have to restart the Ethereum application. This is a rather common problem that can occur, but it can be solved rather easily.

Step 6 to Using Ethereum: Understand Your Main Account Address

When you're working within any blockchain network, you're not going to have a username similar to when you're using an Instagram or Snapchat account. Unlike these types of applications where your identity is integral to the application's function, Ethereum attempts to protect the identities of its users.

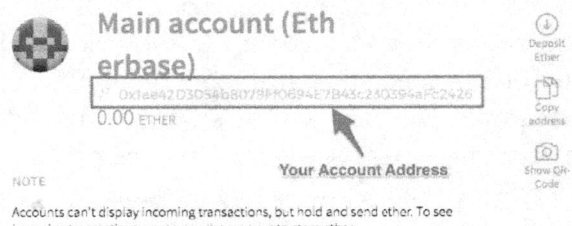

As you can see from the image above, your account address will be a long string of numbers, rather than anything that is easily identifiable.

Step 7 to Using Ethereum: Send Ether to Others

When you know the account address of someone else on the Ethereum network with whom you want to do business, sending money to them is incredibly simple. Click "Send" at the top of your account menu, and then type in the address of the receiver's account. Next, choose how much money you're going to give them. Keep in mind that you're going to have to pay a small transaction fee to the miners who are going to be processing this transaction for you. This will typically be only a small amount of ether, and your transaction should be completed within about thirty seconds. After deciding on the amount that you're going to be sending, you can hit the "Send" button. There is one last step. In order to completely finish the transaction, you must enter your account password. This helps to ensure that you are truly making the decisions for your account.

Step 8 to Using Ethereum: Look at All of Your Past Transactions

As with any blockchain-operated application, Ethereum has a public ledger that everyone on the network can see. If you want to see all of your previous transactions, all you have to do is to go to Wallet overview and then Latest Transactions.

The steps that were presented in this chapter should have been able to walk you through how to operate the Ethereum wallet and user interface. Hopefully, you now feel as if the process involved with setting up Ethereum and using it to trade currency with other people is rather straightforward. We have not yet discussed how to use Smart Contracts. That's because that will be the subject of the following chapter.

Chapter 4: Smart Contracts and Ethereum Integration

Now that you know a bit more about how the Ethereum application operates, you should feel comfortable navigating the Ethereum dashboard and sending and receiving ether. This next chapter is going to get into how you can go about designing your own Smart Contracts on the Ethereum platform. To reiterate, a Smart Contract promises its users efficiency and censorship by only activating when certain parameters within a specific contract have been met. Let's take a look at how these Contracts work, and what they're all about.

Externally-Owned Accounts Versus Contract Accounts

The previous chapter focused solely on externally-owned accounts. In other words, externally-owned accounts are those that are able to send and receive currency. In an externally-owned account, a private encryption key protects the Ethereum wallet from being hacked, by essentially verifying that the sender did in fact intend to send the funds or messages that are being transferred. There is no overarching code that has been programmed into an externally-owned transaction, and the sender in an externally-owned transaction must sign off on the validity of the transaction through their private key before it is completed. This is done by verifying that the nonce number from the transaction matches the nonce number that the sender has sent the receiver.

Contrastingly, a contracts account is one that has a predetermined code already programmed into it. Once the code has been programmed into the contract, the contract itself can then receive messages based on the contract parameters. For example, let's say that you're trying to buy a home. There are many legal documents that must be acquired and signed prior to the mortgage being officially transferred to another person. Within Ethereum, you would be able to send messages to a mortgage contract. With each message that you send, Ethereum would use its storage space (through its swarms, remember?), and accumulate the messages for the contract. Once all the parameters within the contract have been met, the contract will then activate and be seen as completed.

While the previous example made it seem like a project can be completed within a single instance, it's important to understand that a Smart Contract is a *working* document. For example, let's say that you rent an apartment and your landlord has decided to use a Smart Contract for the lease agreement. You make your monthly payments to him/her with ether, and everything is running smoothly. One month, however, you are unable to make your rent payment on time because you had an expensive car repair for which you needed to pay. In fact, you don't have the money to pay your rent for a full seven days after the first of the month. Within the Smart Contract to which you agreed, there is a clause stating that if you do not make your rent payment within five days of the first of the month, you will be charged a $25 late fee. This means that once the sixth of the month comes, the Smart Contract automatically is able to recognize that you have not yet paid your rent and will automatically charge you the appropriate late fee.

While paying a late fee will more than likely be inconvenient for a tenant, the Smart Contract is able to make the job of the landlord much easier. A Smart Contract eliminates the human aspects of being a landlord that include having an awkward conversation with the tenant and demanding the late fee. Additionally, the landlord does not have the keep track of how many days have passed since the tenant was supposed to pay his or her rent. In this way, you should be able to see how a Smart Contract is a living document that does not simply stop working as soon as its parameters have been met. Instead, it acts more like an employee of a business or a clerk whose job it is to keep track of when people are in violations of their contracts. This can be an incredibly useful function. This example also demonstrates how a Smart Contract becomes the middleman that was a lawyer or a realtor in the past. The image below should be able to contextualize these examples a bit more concretely:

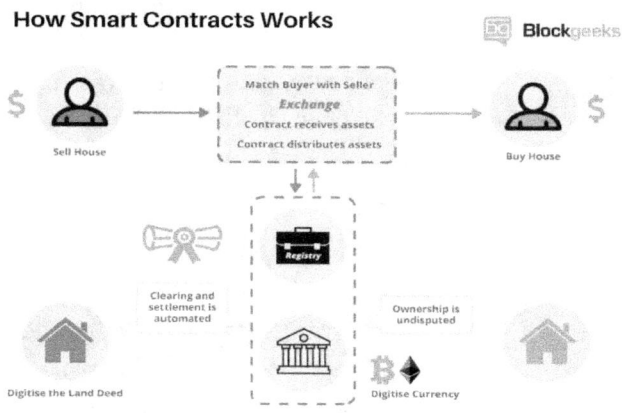

The Benefits of a Smart Contract

We've already discussed how Ethereum in general and Smart Contracts are able to reinforce trust with its users, and have also briefly touched on how Smart Contracts are able to eliminate potential middlemen. Those are two big benefits of Smart Contract implementation, but there are plenty of others that still need to be spelled out. These benefits include:

1. **Duplicity:** The public ledger on any blockchain system is an asset to a Smart Contract in the sense that you don't have to worry about losing your contract or having your information deleted. If something were to happen to your Contract, all of the other users on the network would see your Contract, and would be able to identify it as valid and true.

2. **Speed:** In the world before Smart Contracts, you would often have to wait for banks to process your funds or for paperwork to be processed by other legal entities. With a Smart Contract, your contract can be processed within minutes.

3. **Avoiding Human Error:** Human error often comes when many forms are being filled out by multiple people. With the code within a Smart Contract being written by one person, there is less human error altogether.

4. **Safe:** The blockchain system of cryptography that includes private keys, public keys, and ledgers, makes it difficult for a hacker to infiltrate a contract that's been put in place. This makes a Smart Contract arguably safer than a regular contract, because there are less eyes on what's going on and less potential for ill-willed human motivations to become involved.

Chapter 5: Becoming Acquainted with How Ethereum is Mined

If you're not savvy with computer programming, it does not necessarily mean that you won't be able to figure out how to mine ether. That's what this chapter will cover. After reading this chapter, you will know the steps to take if you ever want to mine ether for yourself. This way, you will not only be familiar with how it's done, but will also be able to follow this process if and when you want to avoid simply purchasing ether from an approved location. Learning how to mine ether will allow you to become more acquainted with everything involved in how Ethereum works.

Step 1 to Mining Ether: Download Geth

Geth stands for "Go Ethereum". To install, you first need to make sure that you're downloading for your appropriate computer. There are other programs that you can download to mine ether, but Geth is a great one to consider because it has been audited to ensure it's safe and secure. Additionally, this program can be used in conjunction with the Ethereum Mist wallet, which we've already discussed in detail.

Once you find the appropriate Geth file for your computer, you will see that it will be downloaded to your computer in a zip file. Unzip it and transfer these files to somewhere on your hard drive where they can be easily accessed. Next, open up the command prompt on your computer. If you're unfamiliar with the command prompt, all you have to do is simply type "CMD prompt" into your computer's search tab. The command prompt is going to look similar to the image below:

Step 2 to Mining Ether: Configuring Your Command Prompt

Once your command prompt is open, the next step is to type information into it. Below is what you should be programming into the command prompt:
C:\Users\Username>
Cd/
C:\>Geth account new

It's important to understand that if the username on your computer has already been set up, that username is going to appear in the "username" section of the prompt. Additionally, you're going to want to press enter after each command that has been entered in code above. Lastly, the "C:" aspects of the code are going to populate by themselves; there's no need to type in these letters, colons, and slashes.

Step 3 to Mining Ether: Create Your Password

Once you commanded Geth to provide you with a new account, you will then be prompted to provide a password for the program. Once you've typed in your password, press enter once more. It may also be a good idea to physically write down your password or keep it in a safe place in case you need to remember it at a later time.

Step 4 to Mining Ether: Download Ethereum

While we've already discussed how you can download Ethereum without seeking to mine, another way to download Ethereum is through your computer's command prompt. If you know that you'd like to mine ether, you should consider downloading Ethereum through the following command prompts:
Geth-rpc

Remember to be patient while Ethereum's blockchains are uploaded to your computer. Once Ethereum has been downloaded to your computer, you have the necessary network for mining capabilities.

Step 5 to Mining Ether: Get Yourself Some Mining Software

Once Ethereum has been downloaded to your computer, you can then work towards integrating mining software that can be used with it. To do this, you have a few options in terms of which program to use. A few of the best mining software programs to use with Ethereum include Ethminer, Genoil, and Claymore. You can use any of these and will still be able to continue with the steps in this chapter. Download the mining software of your choosing before moving onto step 6.

Step 6 to Mining Ether: Initiate the Mining Process

Once the mining software has been downloaded to your computer, open up a new command prompt. From here, type in the following code. Remember to click the enter key on your keyboard after each line of code below has been inputted:
C:\Users\Username>
Cd prog and the tab key

Once you've pressed the tab key once, press it again. This will then display the following code:
C:/>cd "Program files"

Next, press enter. What this has done is given you access to your program files within your command prompt. To gain access to your mining software within the command prompt, type in the following code underneath of the program files command:
Cd cpp

Next, press enter. If you've followed all of the steps correctly up until this point, once you press enter you will see the following code:
C:\Program Files\cpp-ethereum>

Press enter again, and then type in the following:
Claymore-G

This code will vary depending on the exact mining program that you're using. If you're using one that is different than Claymore, simply replace Claymore with the appropriate program name.

Step 7 to Mining Ether: Allow the Mining Process to Begin

Once you've gotten to this point, your computer will be ready to start mining ether. This is going to take a considerable amount of time. First, your computer will need to build what's known as a DAG (Directed Acyclic Graph), which will allow your computer to become ASIC resilient. ASIC stands for Application Specific Integrated Circuits. To store these, your computer is going to require a lot of storage space. For this reason, it would be smart to make sure that your computer has enough storage for these capabilities. Typically, you will need at least 4 GB of RAM in order to mine ether. Of course, the more blockchains that are uploaded to Ethereum, the more laborious it will become for your computer to store all of its information. For this reason, it might be a good idea to either purchase or build a computer specifically designated for ether mining. Otherwise, you could end up running into storage problems in the future.

Mining via Proof of Work

If you're familiar with Bitcoin at all, then you already know that bitcoins are primarily mined through what are known as a Proof of Work (or POW). This function can be best described as an equation that miners must solve in order to produce that nonce number that we've already discussed. The proof of work equation that must be solved by a miner is known as a hash function. In both Bitcoin and Ethereum, the hash function used to secure the mining network is known as the SHA-256 tag. This function can be seen below:

Hash256(d)=SHA-256(SHA-256(d))

In this particular hash function, SHA stands for Secure Hash Algorithm. This means that this function is seeking to protect the blockchain through cyber encryption methods. The "d" variable represents the single transactions that are being processed between users on the Ethereum network.

As long as you pay attention to detail, the process of enabling your computer to mine ether is fairly straightforward. It's advised that you at least have some prior programming knowledge prior to making the decision that you're going to mine your own ether. Lastly, it's important to be careful when you're inputting information into your computer's command prompt. While there's nothing too risky being inputted into it through the mining process, the command prompt is an important place where the wrong information could end up jeopardizing the functionality of your computer.

Chapter 6: Ethereum Versus Bitcoin

At this point in the book, we have discussed all of the major aspects of Ethereum use from a computational and userability perspective. Now that you know about all of the major elements of Ethereum and how to access all of the major aspects of it, we will now turn our attention to focusing on the current climate of blockchain technology from a business perspective. This chapter will focus on how Ethereum differs from Bitcoin, and will also discuss what the current climate is surrounding Ethereum versus Bitcoin.

Bitcoin Giving Blockchain Technology a Name

When bitcoin was first introduced, it was seen as an innovative way for people to make payments and send money online without the use of a middleman or any third party interference. Overtime, however, there have been known problems with bitcoin technology. These problems include hackers infiltrating the bitcoin system and stealing thousands of dollars in bitcoin from its users. In the past, bitcoin has been known to attract people who are looking to sell products on the "black market". This means that criminals have looked to bitcoin as a way to sell products that are illegal in nature. For this reason, multiple countries including Saudi Arabia, Ecuador, and Bolivia have banned the use of bitcoin within its borders.

While bitcoin has its fair share of potential problems, the fact that it was the first blockchain cryptocurrency should not be ignored or overlooked; however, similar to the VHF video tape or the tape player, once the first of a new technology has been introduced, people will likely try to better it or advance it in some fashion. This seems to be the case for Bitcoin. Today, many people recognize the limiting factors of Bitcoin. Instead of trying to better the Bitcoin application itself, many innovators have instead sought to better the technology behind Bitcoin. This is the blockchain. It's important to understand that the problems that exist within bitcoin are problems that are intrinsic to the Bitcoin platform running on top of the blockchain.

Bitcoin as a Springboard for Ethereum Development

In addition to being the first blockchain cryptocurrency to exist, Bitcoin also can only function when currency is being traded between various parties. This is where Ethereum primarily differs from Bitcoin. As we already know, Ethereum expands the functionality of cryptocurrency by allowing people to not just trade currency with one another, but also trade goods through Smart Contracts or subcurrencies that the individual Ethereum user can create on his or her own. It can be argued that this makes Ethereum and Bitcoin similar in one important way – each application is the first of its kind underneath of the cryptocurrency umbrella, respectively. Bitcoin was the first currency trading blockchain platform, while Ethereum was the first beyond-currency trading blockchain platform; however, this comparison should not exclude the fact that without the development of Bitcoin, Ethereum would likely not exist. This fact positions Bitcoin as an integral aspect of blockchain technology development, regardless of Bitcoin's found shortcomings.

How Bitcoin and Ethereum Differ

Even though the importance of Bitcoin as a starting point for Ethereum should not be overlooked, there are still key differences between the two applications. Let's take a look at some of these differences now:

Difference 1: It's Intended Use

When Bitcoin was first developed, it's main purpose was to serve as a coin that could not be regulated by the federal government. If you remember, it was developed during a time when the regulatory banks could not be trusted as a money-governing entity. Ethereum's purpose is to serve as a "world computer". To this end, it's intended purpose is multifaceted and can prove to be useful to many different types of people with many different end goals.

Difference 2: Its User Base

Because of its intended use, it's been proven that both Ethereum and Bitcoin cater to different types of audiences. Users of Bitcoin are typically looking for a network that is completely devoid of authority. There is no central "administrator". On the other hand, Ethereum requires that its users pay a central administrative entity through a small mining transaction fee in order to use its platform. While Ethereum is charging more for users to use its services than Bitcoin, it's important to remember the types of people who have been known to gravitate towards bitcoin. When there is an administrative entity that can dictate what's going on within the blockchain, it's likely that less riffraff or foulplay will occur.

Difference 3: Transaction Pace

The time it takes for a single Bitcoin blockchain to be uploaded to the Bitcoin network is ten minutes. The time for a single Ethereum blockchain to upload is ten seconds. This has been a problem for Blockchain in the past, because this makes it more difficult for the application as a whole to process an infinate number of transactions efficiently.

Difference 4: The Code Type

Bitcoin is designed for the computer programming language known as C++. Contrastingly, Ethereum uses a language known as Turing-Complete. This language is comprised of a whopping seven differently programming language types, including Go, Rust, Haskell, Javascript, Java, Python, and C++. This difference speaks to the universality of Ethereum, because programmers with all different types of backgrounds are able to operate within it.

Difference 5: Evolving Hash Functions

As we already discussed, both Bitcoin and Ethereum currently use POWs to protect their networks; however, Ethereum is currently working towards operating on what's known as a Proof-of-Stake (PoS) blockchain. The reason why Ethereum is seeking to move towards a PoS blockchain is because the cost associated with running a POW blockchain is rather high and inefficient. Additionally, for the lower price that it costs to run a PoS, the developers of Ethereum believe that they will be able to provide their users with a higher level of security than a POW can provide.

Difference 6: Ability to Grow

From its onset, Bitcoin was not developed to grow at the fast rate at which it did. This has led to various problems within the Bitcoin application, most notably, it not being able to keep up with the demand for the product. On the other hand, Ethereum was designed with growth in mind. Currently, Bitcoin is trying to play catchup in this regard.

The most important difference between Ethereum and Bitcoin is arguably that you can implement Smart Contracts using Ethereum, but that has already been discussed in this book. Hopefully, this chapter has provided you with valuable information regarding not just how Ethereum and Bitcoin differ, but also the current climate of how Ethereum plans to evolve and how Bitcoin seems to be falling a tad behind in a few key ways.

Chapter 7: Investing in Ethereum

If you've been reading this book as an attempt to understand the ins and outs of Ethereum without necessarily desiring to start using Ethereum, then you may find this chapter particularly useful. This chapter is going to discuss how you can invest in Ethereum as a company, rather than exclusively participate in buying ether and creating Smart Contracts. We will also discuss the growth of Ethereum as a stock, as well as discuss the risk involved when thinking about making an Ethereum investment.

The Fluctuation in Ethereum's Stock Price

When Ethereum was first brought to the stock market, it was valued at $8 a share. Since January of 2017, this $8 figure has risen to an impressive $350 per share at one point. It's important to note that Bitcoin's stock market price was also valued at $2,300 per share in May of 2017. These numbers suggest that investors have a salivating curiosity for the potential of blockchain platforms. While these prices are certainly impressive, it has not been exclusively an uphill climb for Ethereum's stock. For example, in June 2017 the stock price fell from $319 to just 10 cents in mere seconds, and has also recently been in steady decline since July. Its current market price is set at $199.92.

One of the most critical reasons why blockchain-dominated applications such as Ethereum have seen such a large swing in their stock market prices is because it is still difficult to anticipate whether or not blockchain technology is going to become the way of the future. The people who are investing in Ethereum are doing so rather preemptively, with the hope that blockchain technology will soon dominate the way in which we process contracts and formal documents. For this reason, it cannot be stated outright whether or not you should invest in Ethereum. You will have to make this decision based on your own individual interpretation of the technology and where you think it's ultimately headed.

Reasons Why Investors are Choosing Ethereum

Of course, just because you ultimately have to make this decision on your own, you should still be as informed as possible prior to making this decision. Below are some important reasons why investors are choosing to invest in a technology that still has quite a long way to go in terms of revolutionary impact on the world:

Investors are Choosing to Invest in Ethereum as a Way to Diversify

A good investor should always be looking to diversify his or her portfolio. The cryptocurrency market in general is one that is quite different from any other ones that currently exist. This can be perceived as either a positive or a negative aspect, depending on your outlook. If your glass is half full, you may see the potential for Ethereum to be able to completely change the way in which people interact with certain businesses. The high market share price may also be causing you to think that there is potential for large growth within this sector. On the other hand, what if this high price is only for the short term? What if someone comes along and figures out how to completely break the mathematical algorithms that help blockchain systems to operate? Additionally, it's important to keep in mind that cryptocurrencies are completely unregulated (at least for the time being). This means that the rules are vague, and legality is just as vague. Either way, investing in cryptocurrency will certainly diversify an investor's portfolio.

Cryptocurrencies are Becoming Less Volatile

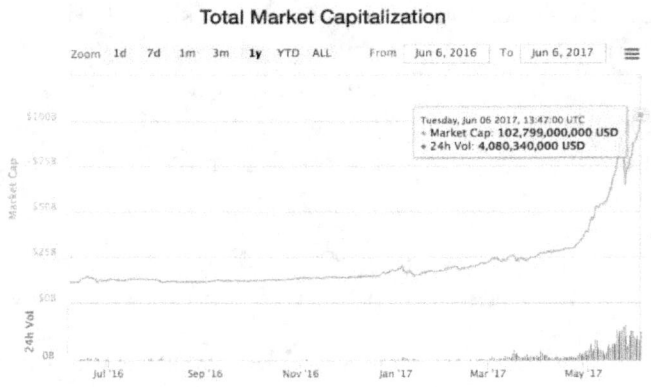

While the risks that were just presented in the previous section are certainly valid, it's important to understand that cryptocurrencies have been being traded on the stock market for quite some time. As you can see from the graph above, cryptocurrency stock has also seen a significant rise in price within the last year. The relatively recent shift in stock price within the last year can largely be attributed to investors being unsure about where the cryptocurrency market as a whole is headed. As new problems arise that need to be hashed out, there are plenty of tweaks that still need to be made within the industry as a whole; however, compared to the past, this volatility is arguably less than when Bitcoin and Ethereum first began being traded on the stock market.

Additionally, the volatility that was largely seen in Ethereum's share price in May 2016 has been seen as both a positive and negative occurrence within the investment industry. To some, the volatility is seen as an opportunity to investors who can capitalize on frequent price changes. To others, this fluctuation appears to be a sign that the cryptocurrency market is experiencing a bubble that is sure to pop once demand becomes too high and the new blockchain applications like Bitcoin and Ethereum cannot keep up. A major reason why the optimistic investors believe that Ethereum's share price will level out is because of their desire to switch to the Proof of Stake function that we discussed earlier. With more security and less money being spent on having to secure the network as a whole, it's been surmised by some that Ethereum's share price will level out and become more consistent as well.

This is an Entirely New Investment Opportunity

Lastly, many investors recognize that investors of the past have never had an opportunity such as the one that cryptocurrency and blockchain technology is presenting right now. Unlike other types of products, people seem to be interested in the future of blockchain technology even though the technology itself has yet to be fully developed. This makes Ethereum and other types of blockchain applications a unique type of investment. Who knows, maybe one day investors will look back and scoff at the $190 share price of Ethereum's stock, because it has only grown in price since its tumultuous days.

This chapter should have made you become aware of the fact that blockchain technology has brought a unique situation upon the investment community. If you're someone who is looking to diversify their investment portfolio, then blockchain technology seems to be a perfect way to achieve this goal; however, it's also important to understand the risks that are involved in this relatively new technology type. If blockchain does not take off and become a revolutionary tool of the future, your investment could end up being a total flop. Because the climate surrounding investing in Ethereum often changes, you should be doing constant research and keeping up with the progression of its investment potential as much as you can prior to making the decision to invest your money in this manner. It might be risky now, but one day your decision to invest in Ethereum could end up being your biggest payday to date.

Chapter 8: Top Tips to Make Your Ethereum Experience Better

If you're not too interested in investing in the future of Ethereum technology, and are more interested in using Ethereum correctly, then you will probably want to know about how you can optimize your Ethereum experience. That is what this chapter will cover. This chapter will get into some of the nuances that exist within the Ethereum application that can take your experience to the next level. If you can avoid mistakes that others have made before you, why wouldn't you seek to do so?

Top Tip 1 for Ethereum Users: Recognize Ethereum's Shortcomings

One of the first tips from which any Ethereum user can benefit is to recognize the current limitations of Ethereum. Sure, the potential *appears* to be on the horizon for Ethereum and its Smart Contracts, but it still has a long way to go before this application should be considered foolproof and completely legitimate. Some of the current problems surrounding Ethereum include the following: scaling to meet demand, figuring out how to audit people properly, and how to properly manage an increasingly growing network. If you approach Ethereum as if everything within its digital borders has been completely figured out, you're simply not looking at the technology realistically and will run the risk of making mistakes with your ether based on those assumptions.

Top Tip 2 for Ethereum Users: Know Some Programming

If you're a noob when it comes to programming, it might not be a good idea to jump into using Ethereum blindly. Before you start using Ethereum, it's recommended that you at least have a basic understanding of how Javascript works. If this does not seem like an immediate possibility for yourself, it might be a good idea to at the very least find a friend who you trust and can walk you through the basics of Ethereum or work on the network on your behalf.

Top Tip 3 for Ethereum Users: Keep Yourself Educated

This cannot be overstated. When thinking about Ethereum as a global technology that can connect people internationally through decentralization, there are multiple facets of society that need to be working together. For example, complete implementation of Ethereum in society will require not just the storage and technical capabilities from thousands of computers to be used as mining stations; it will also require much more. Most notably, the question of how governments will deal with the infrastructure costs needed to make Ethereum viable on a national and global scale is one that is still unanswered. Keeping track of how governments of all shapes and sizes are responding to Ethereum and other blockchain technologies in general will allow you to better understand where Ethereum is headed and how you fit into this larger networking scheme.

Top Tip 4 for Ethereum Users: Always Check Before You Send

Whenever you're sending ether to a new party, you're going to want to make sure that everything seems to be valid prior to sending large amounts of currency. To do this, simply send over a small amount of ether to whomever is receiving it, prior to sending any large amount. This will help to ensure that you're not being duped, and that everything is checking out as it should be. Sure, Ethereum appears to be safer than Bitcoin, but that does not mean that shady characters do not exist on the Ethereum network. You never know who the other person is at the end of your transaction, and this is why it's incredibly important to keep your money as safe as possible.

Top Tip 5 for Ethereum Users: Guard Your Private Key with Your Life

While your public key can be seen by anyone on the Ethereum network, your private key is what fully protects the ether in your wallet. It shouldn't have to be stated, but you'd be surprised at how many people are rather careless with their private key. When you think about the private key as being the secret code that opens up the safe that contains your precious ether, it should be obvious that you need to be extremely careful with it. Some common things that people have been known to do that have led to the infiltration and theft of their Ethereum currency include emailing their private key to someone, posting their private key on social media accounts such as Twitter or Reddit, and storing their private key in their Dropbox. Your email and your Dropbox can be hacked more easily than you think, often through simple phishing techniques, and there is simply no excuse for posting your private key to places where others can see it freely.

Top Tip 6 for Ethereum Users: Make Sure Your Work is Correct

Another simple tip that could end up saving your money is to check your work before sending anything. Similar to when you're transferring money to another account on your computer or posting money to someone on Venmo, an added zero could be the difference between you sending someone ten dollars and one hundred dollars. Within Ethereum, this is even more critical. Sending denominations of currency in decimalized amounts will likely take some getting used to. Along these same lines, it's important to check that the address to which you're sending your currency is correct prior to sending it. It would be a shame to send the wrong person your currency without trying to do so on purpose.

For the tips that were presented in this chapter related to how to use the Ethereum application, the overarching message is to be careful. Beyond the security that you need to put in place for yourself, keeping up with current events that are occuring within and around Ethereum are also incredibly important for multiple reasons. You don't want to invest your dollars into cybercurrency that is going to end up being a dud. For this reason, keep yourself receptive to constantly learning about how Ethereum is evolving. Lastly, remember that this technology is not yet completely developed. For this reason, you will need to steady yourself against setbacks that may come your way, and be as resiliant as possible.

Chapter 9: The Pros and Cons of Ethereum Use

Now that you have a better understanding of how you can protect yourself against fraud within the Ethereum application and are okay with the fact that there are still kinks that need to be worked out within Ethereum as a whole, we will now try to understand both the positive and the negative aspects of what Ethereum can offer you as someone who would like to have a vested interest in Ethereum. This way, you will have a complete and unskewed picture of how Ethereum is perceived and how far it has to go to become a truly global decentralized network.

The Pros of Ethereum

1. **It's Open Source:** Ethereum's software is open source, meaning that any computer programming geek can improve or change its source code. Bitcoin operates in a similar manner. If you're someone who is good and passionate about programming, this could prove to be very useful and advantageous. Additionally, this also allows companies who wish to work together through Ethereum do so. All these companies have to do is hire people on each end who will then program their code to meet their own unique needs as two separate entities merging. Imagine the potential that exists for this type of collaboration.

2. **The EEA Was Recently Created:** We've already discussed the fluctuation of the Ethereum price point on the stock market. Some analysis suggests that a big reason for this recent volatility is because important players have recently decided to invest in what Ethereum has to offer. Some of these entities include Microsoft, Cisco Systems, and JP Morgan. From these names alone, you can tell that these investments are no joke. If corporations like Microsoft and banks with as broad a scope as JP Morgan have made the decision to look more closely at Ethereum, there is reason to believe that Ethereum could end up shifting our society in some key ways. Not only have these companies made the decision to invest in Ethereum, they have gone further by opting to create a partnership known as the Enterprise Ethereum Alliance, or EEA. The three aforementioned companies that have partnered with one another are not the only ones to have done so. Below you will see an image of just some of the other companies who are working within the EEA:

As you can see, this list is nothing to scoff at. As more and more global corporations stake a vested interest in what Ethereum is doing, the potential for its growth will be almost unstoppable.

3. **Exponential Growth:** The open source nature of Ethereum combined with the fact that multiple companies can work together within it allows for infinate growth possibilities. Each time a new project within Ethereum is built and agreed upon, this allows for a new number of potential options for people within Ethereum as a whole to not only use the capabilities that came with the project's addition, but also grow new projects based on the project that was newly created. Infinate growth is truly an exciting possibility, and opens the door for innovative and tranformative growth.

The Cons of Ethereum

Now that we've looked at a few of the advantages that come with the development of Ethereum, let's now look at some of the disadvantages. This way, you will have a complete picture of how Ethereum is currently perceived, from both a positive and negative perspective.

1. **The Inability to Operate Under Risky Code:** One of the key cons that Ethereum is currently facing has to do with its inability to run code that is not entirely trusted. When code is trusted, there is no fear that a transaction will cause all of Ethereum's other safe networks to crash; however,

when code that is being uploaded to the blockchain is untrusted, there is fear that it could cause an entire meltdown of the entire Ethereum blockchain. If you recall, Ethereum uses what's known as a Turing-complete programming language, which allows for an integration of different programming languages. This is why their network is seen to be unsafe for some. Contrastingly, Bitcoin does not use a Turing-complete language, which some will argue makes it a safer application than Ethereum from a code perspective.

2. **Desire for Complexity:** The internet itself was created with simplicity in mind, because simplicity makes it easier to detect foul play. Many people believe that Ethereum should be following the internet's lead. As it stands now, Ethereum is a rather complex network from which to run a wallet and exchange money. For this reason, there is a growing concern that it will be relatively easy for ill-willed people to set themselves up within Ethereum without being easily caught. When a network is active, meaning that it is a living and breathing thing that is constantly changing, complexity often becomes the enemy and ultimate destruction of the network itself. Simplicity is how the internet has survived, and the hope is that Ethereum will follow suit in its design choices.

3. **Stunted Growth:** The developers behind Ethereum are ambitious, yet they seem to be having problems with growing Ethereum as ambitiously as they idealize. This problem seems

to be integrated with the complexity of the Ethereum network. In other words, the need for growth is being solved through attempts that are too complex for network viability. If you remember, Bitcoin takes longer to process blocks than does Ethereum; however, the time that it takes for Bitcoin to process its blocks allows for the blocks in all of the chains to become consistent in nature with one another. In other words, each block is converted into congruent pieces of code by the miners during the POW period. Ethereum is skipping the consistency piece of the blockchain, which many people believe is causing a problem the ability to grow and function on a larger scale.

As you can see, there are both important pros and cons that Ethereum can offer both its users and the world. While a growing number of companies have decided that an investment in Ethereum is a good strategy, there are still many problems for Ethereum to overcome that are crucial to its longterm sustainability.

Chapter 10: Ethereum and the Future Potential of Cryptocurrency

The advantages and disadvantages that were presented in the previous chapter brings to question the future implications of what Ethereum can offer the world. That will be the subject of this chapter. This chapter is going to go into more detail regarding the Proof of Stake migration that Ethereum is seeking to make, and will also discuss what speculators think the future of Ethereum will hold. After reading this chapter, you will have a complete picture of what Ethereum is all about, and what its future holds.

Migration Towards a Proof of Stake Function

As we've already discussed, Ethereum has plans to migrate away from the Proof of Work functions that are currently being used, and towards Proof of Stake functions. By examining how a proof of stake function works, it will become more clear as to why Ethereum is seeking to make this transition. While proof of work needs physical pepole solving equations behind a computer in order to operate, proof of stake does not. The incentive for miners to solve proof of work equations lies in the fact that they're compensated depending on how quickly the equation is solved. The problem with the proof of work function is that it requires trial and error. This is time and resources wasted because it takes on average about ten minutes to solve just one of these equations.

A proof of stake function does the math part automatically. Instead of having miners who will be noded along Ethereum's blockchain network, these people will be known as validators. By watching the blocks that are being created by completion of the algorithms that are being automatically generated, a validator can then bid on blocks that he or she believes should be added to the blockchain. Of course, this requires first that a validator has bought ether to spend for the bidding process. Let's name a fictional validator Hank. Hank watches the blockchains that are being created and decides to bid some ether on one. He then watches to see whether or not this particular block has been added to the chain. It turns out that he was right, and so he is rewarded in ether for the bid that he placed on his winning block; however, if Hank had been incorrect, his original bid would have been swallowed by the network. As you can see, instead of being motivated by competition to complete the algorithms as quickly as possible through proof of work, proof of stake incentivizes through gambling.

To transition towards proof of stake, Ethereum plans to slowly integrate proof of stake into its current system. Once initiated, most of Ethereum is going to still operate through proof of work, but a small fraction of the transactions on the network will be completed through proof of stake. This way, Ethereum will be able to test whether or not the proof of stake method of block verification is going to work within the current Ethereum database construction.

The Four Phases of Ethereum Growth

From its onset, Ethereum was planned to function within four areas of growth. You can think of these phases as being similar to new Smartphone updates. You receive these updates because the code for the phone has been enhanced. These phases work similarly. The four areas are as follows:

1. The Frontier Phase: This was the first launch of Ethereum.
2. The Homestead Phase: This is current phase of Ethereum as of 2017.
3. The Metropolis Phase: This is the next phase that people are anticipating to be launched rather soon.
4. The Serenity Phase: This is the final phase of Ethereum.

The Metropolis Phase

There are a variety of enhancements that the metropolis phase will introduce. These enhancements have been decided upon with the eventual goal of having Ethereum become a platform that is invisible to all uninformed eyes. In other words, people will be using programs that run on top of the Ethereum blockchain, but the breadth of Ethereum is so expansive that only the technically savvy understand that Ethereum is running the application in question. These enhancements are as follows:

1. **The Introduction of zk-snarks:** Zk-snarks is an acronym which stands for Zero Knowledge Succinct Non-interactive Argument of Knowledge. Without getting into too much

detail, Zk-snarks is basically a way for someone who is sending money within Ethereum to prove to the receiving party that they truly possess certain information or value. It's a security measure that would heighten Ethereum's ability to protect its users.
2. **Providing Greater Freedom for Smart Contracts:** In the future, Smart Contracts will be able to collect fees related to their contracts automatically, without prompting a person who is privy to the contract to do so.
3. **Greater Anonymity:** In pursuit of Ethereum's goal of eventually becoming invisible to the public eye, developers are working towards enabling their users to be able to use other types of crytpocurrency within Ethereum's borders. This includes bitcoin.
4. **Additional Enhancements:** Ethereum refers to additional features that will enhance various aspects of Ethereum's platforms. These are referred to as EIPs, Ethereum Improvement Protocols.

As you can see, Ethereum itself recognizes that it has strides to make before it can cerifiably state that it's finished its development process. In fact, it has been designed to mature over a long period of time. The reasoning behind this is because the developers wanted to have adequate time to develop the technology during each phase of its maturation, without having to rush to completion. When you think about the fact that the developers at Ethereum actually planned to introduce this application over a longer period of time, it can also possibly allude to the notion that Ethereum is an application that will eventually integrate itself into our society in permanent and revolutionary ways. It seems as if the public is less patient than the people behind the platform itself. This is why it's important to carefully examine the implications of Ethereum and be on the lookout for its developments in the future.

Conclusion

Thank you for making it to the end of this book, *Investing in Ethereum: A Simple, Concise & Complete Guide to Investing in the New Cryptocurrency Ethereum*. Hopefully, this book has provided you with great insight on how you can start investing in Ethereum cryptocurrency. With all of the great benefits that Ethereum can offer, especially in terms of transparency and decentralization, there's no doubt that you could benefit from investing your money into this relatively new platform. It's still questionable as to whether or not the future of money is paper or digital; yet, with credit cards and digital transaction methods such as Venmo becoming increasingly popular, you definitely do not want to miss out on at least attempting to invest in Ethereum. It's that simple.

The next step is to start thinking about how you're going to create your own Ethereum network and also consider downloading an Ethereum Wallet for yourself. Even if you don't think that you'd ever use Ethereum to start your own network, it still may be beneficial for you to own some ether of your own. With companies such as Microsoft heavily interested in what Ethereum can offer the world, it's clear that large corporations have a vested interest in developing this particular type of cryptocurrency. In addition to reading this book, doing more research is never a poor choice to make. Stay current on what's going on within the blockchain industry, and always make decisions with as many facts as possible.

For useful resources check out:
www.wisereachday.com/ethereum/

Finally, if you enjoyed reading this book, a review on Amazon is always appreciated! Thank you!

www.ingramcontent.com/pod-product-compliance
Lightning Source LLC
Chambersburg PA
CBHW050021230526
45470CB00003B/1065